Celebrating Differences

Different Cultures

by Rebecca Pettiford

Bullfrog Books

Ideas for Parents and Teachers

Bullfrog Books let children practice reading informational text at the earliest reading levels. Repetition, familiar words, and photo labels support early readers.

Before Reading
- Discuss the cover photo. What does it tell them?
- Look at the picture glossary together. Read and discuss the words.

Read the Book
- "Walk" through the book and look at the photos. Let the child ask questions. Point out the photo labels.
- Read the book to the child, or have him or her read independently.

After Reading
- Prompt the child to think more. Ask: What special practices or celebrations are a part of your culture?

Bullfrog Books are published by Jump!
5357 Penn Avenue South
Minneapolis, MN 55419
www.jumplibrary.com

Library of Congress Cataloging-in-Publication Data

Names: Pettiford, Rebecca, author.
Title: Different cultures / by Rebecca Pettiford.
Description: Minneapolis, MN: Jump!, Inc., [2018]
Series: Celebrating differences | Audience: Age 5–8.
Audience: K to grade 3. | Includes index.
Identifiers: LCCN 2016055052 (print)
LCCN 2017006555 (ebook)
ISBN 9781620316696 (alk. paper)
ISBN 9781620317228 (pbk.)
ISBN 9781624965463 (ebook)
Subjects: LCSH: Culture—Juvenile literature.
Classification: LCC GN357 .P48 2018 (print)
LCC GN357 (ebook) | DDC 306—dc23
LC record available at https://lccn.loc.gov/2016055052

Editor: Jenny Fretland VanVoorst
Book Designer: Leah Sanders
Photo Researcher: Leah Sanders

Photo Credits: Dreamstime: Zhaojiankang, 3; Darkbird77, 22tl. Getty: nik wheeler, 1; Jose Luis Pelaez, 5; Tibor Bognar, 10–11; ImagesBazaar, 18–19. iStock: Catherine Lane, cover; Bartosz Hadyniak, 4; SoumenNath, 12–13; Bodhichita, 14–15; NinaHenry, 16; photosbyjim, 17; pushlama, 20–21. Shutterstock: Monkey Business Images, 8, 9, 22br; SMDSS, 13; Anjo Kan, 22tr; 2shrimpS, 22bl; Ovu0ng, 24. Thinkstock: Valueline, 6–7.

Printed in the United States of America at Corporate Graphics in North Mankato, Minnesota.

Table of Contents

Many Ways

We all have different ways.

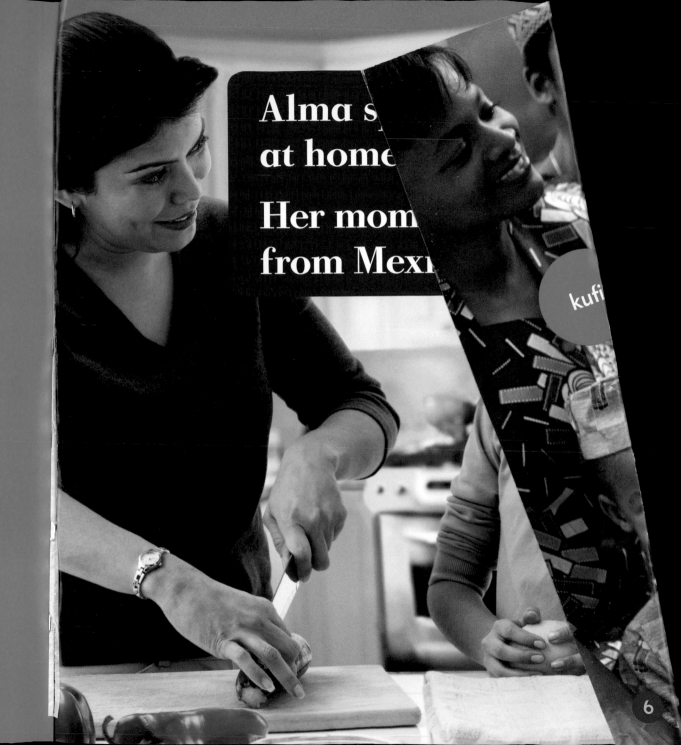

Alma s
at home

Her mom
from Mexi

kufi

It is Kwanzaa.

Marc wears a kufi.

His family
lights candles.

Aki eats sushi.
It is raw fish.

8

It is part of her culture.

sushi

Lilo dances the hula.

It is from Hawaii.

Wow! She is graceful.

It is Diwali.

Nita decorates.

She uses colored sand.

She uses lights.

Look! A flower.

Ben is Amish.

He rides in a buggy.

Why?

His family does
not use a car.

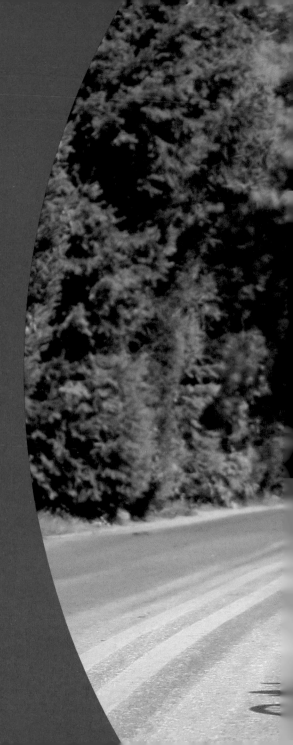

Ty dances at a powwow.

bells

Listen!

He has bells on his ankles.

It is Eid.

Ali's family gives gifts.

They share a feast.

Yum!

19

We all have different ways.

What are some of yours?

Your Ways

Think about some of the different practices mentioned in the book. Then look at the pictures and think of your own culture as you answer the questions.

Is there a special food you eat?

Is there a special dance that is part of your culture?

What holidays do you celebrate?

What language does your family speak?

Picture Glossary

Amish
A Christian group whose members live a traditional way of life.

Eid
Short for Eid al-Fitr, the Muslim holiday that ends the fasting period of Ramadan.

culture
The beliefs and practices of a racial, religious, or social group.

Kwanzaa
An African American holiday that begins December 26 and ends January 1.

Diwali
The Hindu festival of lights held in October or November.

powwow
A Native American festival.

23

Index

To Learn More

Learning more is as easy as 1, 2, 3.

1) Go to www.factsurfer.com

2) Enter "differentcultures" into the search box.

3) Click the "Surf" button to see a list of websites.

With factsurfer.com, finding more information is just a click away.